FIDGET
BUSTERS

By Jolene L. Roehlkepartain

Group
Books

Loveland, Colorado

Dedication

To Dorothy Roehlke, my mom,
who finds the best in each child she meets—
and who found the best in me.

Fidget Busters
Copyright © 1991 Jolene L. Roehlkepartain

Credits
Edited by Cindy S. Hansen and Lois Keffer
Designed by Dori Walker
Computer Graphic Artist: Suzi Jensen

Library of Congress Cataloging-in-Publication Data
Roehlkepartain, Jolene L., 1962-
    Fidget busters / by Jolene L. Roehlkepartain.
      p.   cm.
    ISBN 1-55945-058-4
    1. Amusements. 2. Games. 3. Church work with youth. I. Title.
GV1203.R5827 1991
790.1'922—dc20   91-39909
                                              CIP

14 13 12 11 10 9 8 7   04 03 02 01 00 99 98 97 96

Printed in the United States of America.

Contents

Part Three: Fidget Busters for Fourth- to Sixth-Graders

Part Four: Fidget Busters for Children of All Ages

Introduction

"Where's My Bag of Tricks?"

"Sit still!"

How many times have I said that to children? More often than I'd like to admit. It seems children never stop wiggling, giggling, whispering or looking around. And my be-still commands never seem to work for long.

By nature, children have short attention spans and lots of energy. So how do you help children get the ants out of their pants and learn something? Try this resource full of wiggle-eaters.

Fidget Busters contains quick, fun, easy ideas that are divided into four sections. You get fidget busters for preschoolers, kindergartners to third-graders, fourth- to sixth-graders and children of all ages. Each activity is easy to lead and takes little or no preparation.

Before a lesson, have a few of these ideas ready to go. When the fidgeting starts, stop what you're doing and try one of these fidget busters. Then return to your learning activity with kids who can concentrate.

Here are a few tips for using the activities:

● **Be enthusiastic.** Let your enthusiasm spread. Fidget

busters should be lively and energizing—bright breathers to liven up a sleepy atmosphere.

● **Keep transitions quick.** Get right into and out of an activity. Don't spend a lot of time getting ready. Be prepared. Know what activity you want to use ahead of time.

● **Lead energizing activities that don't put down anyone or make anyone feel inferior.** We are the children of God, so we should at all times "encourage one another and build each other up" (1 Thessalonians 5:11).

● **Include everyone in the activities.** Keep your eyes roving for those who are reluctant to participate. Some kids are more shy than others and need a little extra coaxing to join in.

● **Adapt the activities to fit your group size.** All the ideas in **Fidget Busters** can be used in a small group. If your group has more than six to eight members, form more teams when necessary.

● **Use and adapt the ideas to complement a meeting theme.** If you're studying Samson, play Pillars and Runners (activity 77). If you're studying the good Samaritan, play The Samaritan Shuffle (activity 57). If your meeting theme is about thankfulness, try the Joyful Jog (activity 98).

● **For younger children, demonstrate as you explain an activity.** For example, you take the first turn in a follow-the-leader activity. Use motions such as skipping, clapping, twisting and jumping. Then ask a child to take the lead. Demonstrations make the instructions more understandable.

● **Prepare a game-filled grab bag.** Decorate a paper bag by coloring it with markers or crayons. Choose several no-equipment-needed activities for the age group you're working with. Write one activity per 3×5 card. Then place all the cards in the bag. As soon as the wiggles wander into your lesson, pull out the bag and ask a volunteer to choose one activity out of it. Then work on those wiggles. And have a blast!

So instead of working against those wiggles and fidgets, work with them. You'll be glad you did. Because children will pay attention better when you give them short breaks to move around.

PART ONE
Fidget Busters for Preschoolers

Wiggle Worms

Make the most out of kids' wiggles and fidgets during your lesson. Tell kids to imagine that they're all wiggly, squirmy worms. Have them lie on the floor and follow your instructions. Say:

❑ **The worms are all sleeping. What kinds of noises do they make?** (Kids snore or breathe heavily.)

❑ **The worms are waking up now. How would worms stretch to wake up?** (Kids yawn and stretch their arms and legs.)

❑ **The worms are hungry for breakfast. What kinds of noises and actions would worms make when they're eating?** (Kids make chewing noises and use their hands like they're stuffing food into their mouths.)

❑ **The worms are ready to play. How do worms play?** (Kids wiggle around.)

❑ **The worms are Bible bookworms. Let's wiggle back to our seats and get back into the lesson.**

2

Popcorn Popper

(You'll need popcorn for a snack.)

Tell the children they're like kernels of unpopped popcorn. Explain that when you heat popcorn kernels, a few start popping, and after a while, all the kernels are popping.

Have kids crouch on the floor with their heads between their knees. Tell them the popcorn kernels are getting hotter and hotter, and some kernels are beginning to pop. Kids should slowly start to pop by jumping up and yelling "Pop!"—and keep popping. One child may pop on one side of the room while another child on the other side of the room pops. Gradually more kids should begin to pop until all kids are jumping up and down yelling "Pop! Pop!"

Once children have jumped up and down for a while, say: **Let's pop back to our lesson.** Serve popcorn as a snack.

3

Bellybutton Buddies

Say: **Let's run off some energy and play a silly game.** Have children run around the room. When you yell "Bellybuttons," children must quickly find partners and point their fingers to their partners' bellybuttons.

Repeat this activity a number of times, then say: **Now let's all point to our own bellybuttons before getting back to our lesson.**

4

Shadow Dancing

(You'll need music to play.)

On a sunny day, take the children outside to dance with their shadows. (When the weather is too cold, you could play this game indoors by shutting off overhead lights and turning on table lamps.)

Play music and have children do different dance steps with their shadows. Kids could march, twist and wiggle to the tune. After a few minutes, have children pair up to dance with a partner's shadow.

Then say: **My shadow told me it's time to say goodbye so we can get back to our lesson. Say goodbye to your shadow and let's go inside.**

5

Big to Little

When your classroom feels like a zoo, take advantage of it. Ask children to stand in a circle. Then have kids turn so they can follow the person in front of them and walk in a circle. Have children act out a series of animals while walking.

Explain that you're going to call out animal names. Children will act like each animal and make the kind of noise it makes. Call out these animal names:

❑ horse   ❑ dog   ❑ pig
❑ cow   ❑ cat   ❑ bird
❑ monkey   ❑ lion   ❑ mouse

Say: **Choose your favorite animal to act like and sound like as we all go back to our lesson.**

6

Traffic Jam

(You'll need a whistle.)

When you want an attention-getting break, blow on a whistle and say: **Time for a traffic jam. Let's all pretend to be cars.**

Have children run around the room yelling "Honk! Honk!" When you blow your whistle, children screech on their brakes and stop. When you blow the whistle again, they can resume "driving." Continue this stop-and-go motion until your children run out of gas.

Say: **Let's drive back to our lesson and park for a while.**

7

Clothespin Adventure

(You'll need clothespins and markers or crayons.)

Give each child a clothespin to decorate with markers or crayons. Have children draw faces on their clothespins. Then go outside. Explain that you'll read a story about the clothespin friends. As you read the story, have children run to the places you mention and clamp their clothespins onto whatever you name. Adapt the story to your surroundings.

A group of clothespins were best friends. They always stuck together. One day they decided to investigate a tree (pause). **They all ran to a tree and sat on the leaves** (pause) **and branches** (pause). **After they rested for a while, they decided to visit the grass** (pause) **to see who lived there.**

The clothespins liked walking around the grass, but then they saw a playground (pause). **They all liked going down the slide** (pause). **But after going down the slide, they were tired and decided to take a short nap.**

After sleeping for a while, the clothespins yawned and stretched to wake up. They were happy about all the wonderful things outside that God had given them: trees (pause), **grass** (pause), **the playground** (pause). **But best of all, they liked each other** (pause).

Say: **The clothespins want to go back to the lesson. Why don't we join them?**

8

Dinosaur Dance

(You'll need music to play. Pictures of
dinosaurs are optional.)

If you brought dinosaur pictures to class, show them
to the kids, then say: **Let's use our imagina-
tions. Think about dinosaurs—those crea-
tures who used to live long-g-g ago. Let's do
some dinosaur dancing!**

Form groups of three. Designate one person in
each group as the dinosaur's head, the second as the
dinosaur's middle and the third as the dinosaur's tail.
Have groups create a dinosaur dance to show the rest of
the class. Talk about how some dinosaurs were big, so
they could dance using huge, long steps. Some dinosaurs were little, so they could take tiny, tiptoe steps.

Play music and let each dinosaur group dance for
the rest of the children. After all the groups have done
their dances, let all the dinosaurs dance together.

Stop the music and say: **Now let's dance back
to our lesson**.

9

Caught in the Rain

Tell children that they're plants and must stand with their feet firmly on the floor. Without moving their feet, they must react to different kinds of weather like a plant. Then announce these different kinds of weather. Do the actions with them.

❑ rain ❑ sun ❑ breeze
❑ wind ❑ snow ❑ hail

Say: **Let's uproot ourselves and plant ourselves back into our seats to learn more about our lesson**.

10

Uh-Oh!

(You'll need a large cardboard box.)

When you see a mess in the room, use this cleanup activity. Hold up the empty box and say: **Uh-oh, I see toys and things lying around the room. Let's race to pick up everything and put them inside this Uh-Oh Box.**

After everything has been gathered, have children figure out the proper homes for all the items in the Uh-Oh Box. Help children if they don't know where something goes. After everything is put away, say: **Thanks for putting everything away. Uh-oh, I see it's time to get back to our lesson!**

Into the Ark

Choose two children to face each other and hold hands in the air to form an arch between them for other children to go through. Tell the rest of the children that they're animals, and the two children forming the arch are the door to Noah's ark.

Tell children (except for the ones posing as the door to the ark) to run around the room. Then shout: **It's starting to rain. Let's get into the ark two by two.** Help children find partners and decide what animal to be together; for example, two cows, two dogs, two horses or two cats. Then have them act and sound like the animals as they pass under the arch to get into the ark.

Repeat the activity several times so children can take turns being the door to the ark. Then say: **Now that we're all in the ark, let's sail back to our lesson.**

12

Color Race

(You'll need red, blue, green and yellow crayons.)

Play the following game to help kids learn colors as they run off some built-up energy. Hold up a red crayon so kids can see its color. Then say: **Raise your hand if you're wearing red** (pause). Hold up the blue crayon, then say: **Raise your foot if you're wearing blue** (pause). Hold up the green crayon, then say: **Nod your head if you're wearing green** (pause). Hold up the yellow crayon, then say: **Pat your legs if you're wearing yellow** (pause).

Tell children that you'll shout out a color, and they must run and touch something that's that color. After every child has found something that matches the color you shouted, shout out a different color.

Play this activity in a lot of different settings: at a park, in the parking lot, in a Sunday school room, in a nursery.

Then say: **Now let's race back to our colorful lesson.**

13

Spin and Run

(You'll need two plastic 2-liter bottles with
an arrow drawn on each.)

S ay: **Let's have a little spin-and-run fun.**
Form two groups and have each group sit in a
circle. Put a plastic bottle in the middle of each
circle. Have children take turns spinning the bottle.
When the bottle stops spinning and the arrow points at
a child, that child should jump up, run to the other
circle and join that game. Children will constantly be
switching circles.

After a while, say: **Since our heads are all spinning, let's take a break and see what our lesson
says.**

14

Dust and Vacuum

I nterrupt your lesson with a "cleaning" demonstra-
tion. Show how to dust someone (lightly rub in a
circular motion on a person's arm or back) and how
to vacuum someone (rub up and down on a person's
arm or back).

When you yell "dust," children dust each other.
When you yell "vacuum," children vacuum each other.

After a few minutes of cleaning, say: **Now let's
clean up the rest of our lesson.**

15

Rainbow Line

(You'll need a colorful scarf for each child and for yourself.
Place the scarves in a sack. Music is optional.)

Get your kids' attention by holding up the sack
full of colorful scarves. Say: **God gave us
rainbows as a sign of his forgiveness and
love. Ready to make a dancing rainbow?**

Ask kids to stand in a straight line. Place a scarf in
each child's right hand. Then have children join the
line together by grabbing the end of their neighbor's
scarf with their left hands. You hold a scarf, too, and
stand in the front of the line.

You lead the line first. Walk, skip, jump, run, dip,
zigzag and do other movements for the rest of the children to follow. After about a minute, take your scarf
and go to the end of the line so a new person in front
can lead.

After several children have led the actions, take
leadership of the line again and lead kids back to the
meeting area. Have kids sit down. Collect the scarves,
then continue the lesson.

16

Hidden Straws

(You'll need 10 drinking straws.)

Prior to your lesson, hide 10 drinking straws around the room. When kids get restless, invite them to see who can find the most straws. When all 10 straws, have been found, have kids cover their eyes while you hide them again. Play several times.

Then say: **Now that we've found all those straws, let's find our way back to our lesson.**

17

Double Log Roll

Have the children find partners and line up. Tell kids that they're going to pretend they're logs rolling down a hill. Have the first set of partners lie on the floor head to head, and then join hands. Have the pair roll to a point about 10 feet away and return—without letting go of their hands. When the first pair returns, the next pair starts rolling while the first pair goes to the end of the line.

When all the pairs have succeeded, say: **Now let's roll back to our lesson.**

18

Clap, Clap, Stomp, Stomp

Get kids' attention by stopping during your lesson, saying these words and doing the actions: **Clap, clap, stomp, stomp, turn around and jump.**

Invite children to do it with you. Have them mimic the action as they repeat the chant. Do the actions at different speeds—slowly at first for children to catch on.

Then say: **Now let's all clap, clap, stomp, stomp, turn around and jump back to our lesson.**

19

Stop and Smile

Stop what you're doing and take a smile-stretching break. Have children run around the room. Whenever you say "Stop and smile," each child pairs up with another child face to face and smiles. Repeat the activity over and over so children have lots of different partners and the smiles turn to giggles.

Then say: **Let's all keep smiling because we know Jesus loves us. Let's go back to our lesson and learn more about him.**

20

Goodbye, Hello

Stop your lesson and have children each find a partner by grabbing the hand of a person sitting by them. Tell the partners to stand up and go to an area in the room where they can move around.

Explain that when you say "goodbye," partners should run away from each other. When you say "hello," partners should turn around and run toward each other. Switch back and forth often to keep the excitement high.

After a while, keep saying "hello" and have kids each hug their partners. Then say: **Let's say goodbye to this game and hello again to our lesson.**

21

Fix the Room

Say: **Did you know Jesus learned to be a carpenter from his dad, Joseph? Let's pretend we're carpenters and fix up the room.** Have children run to an area you call out and fix it in the way you say. Do the motions with them. For example:

❑ Hammer the floor. ❑ Saw the door.
❑ Measure the window. ❑ Drill the wall.

Then say: **You're all such good carpenters! You'd make Jesus proud. Now let's make noises like drills and drill our way back to our lesson so we can learn more about him.**

22

Rolling Ball

(You'll need several balls of different sizes,
including a beach ball.)

March around the room and say: **Follow me
right now. This way! And you'll see
what game we'll play.**

Have children kneel in a circle with an arm's
length of space between them. Give one child a beach
ball to start rolling across the circle. Have other children keep the ball moving inside the circle by gently
pushing it with their hands. Tell them not to move
from their knees. If the ball leaves the circle or stops
moving, start again.

Once children catch on to the game, add another
different-size ball. Keep both balls rolling around the
circle. Add different balls as long as you want. Then say:
Now it's time to get our lesson rolling again.

23

Kings and Queens of the Mountain

(You'll need several old cushions.)

This activity turns an old competitive game into a new group-builder. Instead of pushing each other down, kids pull each other up.

Put an old cushion on the floor and have kids see how quickly they can get the whole group on top of this "mountain." Gradually add additional cushions and see how quickly the kids can help each other get on top all at once. (Be careful not to pile the cushions too high.)

Then say: **Now that we've reached the mountaintop, let's hurry down to get back to our lesson.**

Good Morning

Yawn and stretch in front of everyone. Then say: **Oh, I'm so tired. Let's go lie down on the floor.** Tell kids that you'll take them through a refreshing, relaxing morning routine and they should act out your instructions. (Do the actions with them.)

❑ The alarm goes off—turn off the alarm.
❑ Stretch in bed.
❑ Roll out of bed.
❑ Shuffle slowly to the bathroom.
❑ Turn on the light.
❑ Brush your teeth.
❑ Comb your hair.
❑ Walk back to your room.
❑ Put on your clothes.
❑ Fold your pajamas.
❑ Walk to the kitchen.
❑ Say a prayer.
❑ Eat breakfast.

Then say: **We're running late. Let's run to our lesson and learn more.**

25

Lost in the Blizzard

(You'll need a blindfold for each child.)

Toss a blindfold to each person. Say: **Here, catch!**
Ask children to spread out around the room,
then blindfold them. Explain that everyone is
lost in a snowy blizzard and can't see. However, children can yell for help and find other children in the
blizzard by following the sounds of their voices.

Tell children that you don't want anyone left
stranded in the blizzard, so as soon as they find another
child, they should hold hands and try to link up with
more children. (Help hesitant children find the others.)

When all the children have linked up together, say:
**We all found each other! Good! Now let's take
off our blindfolds and see what we can find in
the rest of our lesson.**

PART TWO

Fidget Busters for Kindergartners to Third-Graders

26

Super Spotlights

(You'll need a frying pan, a or similar
shiny object, or a flashlight.)

Do this activity outside when it's sunny. **Say:
Follow me. I want you all to shine in a
lively activity.**

Hold the frying pan (or other shiny object) and
deflect the sunlight onto someone. (If the sun isn't
shining, use a flashlight.) That person must shout out
an activity for the whole group to do (such as 10 jumping jacks or three somersaults.)

After kids have done the activity, give the shiny
object to the person who was in the "spotlight" and let
him or her deflect the sunlight onto another person
who then yells out another activity.

After several kids have been in the spotlight, have
someone shine the sunlight on you. Say: **We're all
done with our fun in the sun. Let's run back to
where we're doing our lesson and take a seat.**

27

Wet and Wild

(You'll need two spray bottles filled with water.)

Cool off on a hot summer day with this variation of tag. You can do this activity indoors or outdoors.

Ask two children to be "It." Give them each a spray bottle filled with water. Explain that the class is stranded on a desert island, and the two "Its" will try to cool off everyone by spraying them.

When a child gets sprayed with water, he or she must sit down. The last two kids to get sprayed become "It" for the next round. Make two rules: no spraying others in the eyes and no drenching others with water— one squirt per person.

After several children have been "It," say: **I'm going to rescue you from this wet island by starting the lesson again.**

28

Sandwiches, Anyone?

(You'll need sandwiches for snacks.)

Number children off by fours. Tell the ones they're bread, the twos they're meat, the threes they're cheese, and the fours they're lettuce.

Explain that the children will make sandwiches (with two pieces of bread on the outside and the proper ingredient on the inside) when you call out a certain kind of sandwich. Kids should hug together to form the sandwich. The extra ingredients cheer the "sandwiches" by saying "Yum! Yum!"

Call out these sandwiches:
❏ meat sandwich
❏ cheese sandwich
❏ meat and cheese sandwich
❏ cheese and lettuce sandwich
❏ lettuce sandwich
❏ bread sandwich

Say: **Now that we've been sandwiches for a while, let's go nibble on our lesson.**

Following the lesson, serve sandwiches for a snack. How about meat, cheese and lettuce sandwiches?

Colorful Tongues

(You'll need four different colors of unprepared,
presweetened Kool-Aid as described in the activity.
You'll also need prepared Kool-Aid and cookies as a snack.)

Have children form four groups. (They don't need to be even in number.) Give each group a different color of unprepared Kool-Aid: red, green, purple or orange. Have children each put a little bit of the Kool-Aid dust on their tongues until their tongues turn that color.

Then have children mingle while they stick out their tongues. Call out colors and have children whose tongues are that color run, form a circle around you, hold hands and skip around you three times. Then have them go back to mingling with the rest of the group.

Call out one color at a time at first. Then call out two colors. Then three. End by calling all four colors.

Serve Kool-Aid and cookies as a snack. Offer a prayer thanking God for his sweet and colorful gift of forgiveness. Then return to your lesson.

Tumbling Down

Form two groups, with one group having a few more children than the other. Have the smaller group of children form a circle and hold hands, facing inward. Then have the larger group form a circle around the smaller group, facing inward.

Tell kids in the middle circle that they live in Jericho and are having a good time. Have them hold hands and skip around the circle. Tell them when they hear the children in the outside circle make trumpet sounds, they have to fall down.

Meanwhile have kids in the larger circle march around the smaller circle. When they've gone around seven times, have them pretend they're playing trumpets—with full sound effects—causing the children in the smaller circle to fall down like the walls of Jericho.

Play the game a few times so children can take turns being walls and trumpeters. Then say: **Let's all march back to our seats to learn more about our lesson.** Read about the walls of Jericho in Joshua 6.

Around in Circles

Say: **Attention everyone! Stand up** (pause). **Turn around in a circle as you shout "Around in circles"** (pause). **Sit back down** (pause). **Now you know what you have to do for a quick little "get-your-blood-circulating" exercise.**

Explain that when you call out a description, all the children who fit that label should do what they just practiced: stand up, turn around, shout "Around in circles" and sit back down.

Call out various descriptions such as all children who:

❑ have brown hair
❑ wear glasses
❑ have a missing tooth
❑ have a sister
❑ have green eyes
❑ like to listen to Bible stories
❑ have freckles
❑ take piano lessons
❑ like the color red

For the last description, say: **Are great kids in this class.** Then continue the lesson after kids are all sitting down.

32

Scripture Scrambler

Tell children a simple Bible verse, such as Matthew 5:9, "Blessed are the peacemakers, for they will be called sons of God." Talk to the kids about what they think a peacemaker is. Ask if they know anyone who is a peacemaker. (Teachers who stop kids from fighting. Police officers who watch out for our safety. We are peacemakers when we play well with our friends.)

Then together with the children, say the verse in each of these ways:

❑ at a normal pace while standing
❑ in fast forward while jogging in place
❑ in a whisper while tiptoeing
❑ shouting while marching
❑ in slow motion while jogging in slow motion
❑ in a normal voice while walking backward

Say: **I'm so proud that you learned this Bible verse. Now let's get back to our lesson to learn even more!**

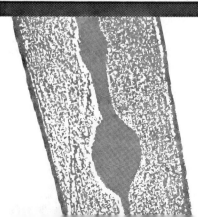

33

Ice-Cube Secret

(You'll need several ice cubes.)

Ask for a volunteer and have him or her leave the room. Have the rest of the children sit in a circle. Then give one child an ice cube to pass around the circle. Tell children to be sneaky in passing the ice cube because the child outside will come in and guess who has the ice cube while it's being passed around.

Invite the child back to the room and have him or her guess who has the ice cube. When he or she guesses correctly, have the child who's holding the ice cube leave the room. Play several times so a lot of children can be the "guessers."

Then say: **Now that our hands are all cold, let's warm up by going back to our lesson.**

34

Pop-Up Prayer

Say: **Let's take some time to say a unique prayer, pop-up style.** Lead kids to a clear area in the room and have them crouch down.

Say: **We're going to thank God for all the wonderful things he has made. When I say a category, jump up and name a specific thing that you're thankful for. I might say a category such as food. You could pop up and say specific things, such as pizza, hamburgers or ice cream. All you need to say is one word and then crouch down again until you think of something else. Ready?**

Then mention the following, pausing after each one:

- ❑ Thanks, God, for colors ...
- ❑ Thanks, God, for toys ...
- ❑ Thanks, God, for food ...
- ❑ Thanks, God, for animals ...
- ❑ Thanks, God, for people ...
- ❑ Thanks, God, for everything. Amen.

Conclude by saying: **Now we can be thankful for our lesson. Let's get back to it.**

35

Count Away

Figure out what items in your room are in multiples; for example, crayons, coats, books and cabinet doors. Then shout out one of these items and have children all run to that area and count the items.

Once children have figured out a total, name another item for children to count. Continue until kids have counted several items.

Then say: **I knew I could count on you to be good counters. Now let's count how many steps it takes to get back to our seats.**

36

Sock Rob

(Bring several pairs of socks.)

Have children all take off their shoes so everyone is stocking-footed. Supply extra socks in case some kids aren't wearing any. Then have everyone sit on the floor. Tell children that the goal is to pull off as many socks as they can while keeping their own on. Explain that everyone must stay seated with their bottoms on the floor during the activity. The only way to move around to rob others' socks is to scoot on their bottoms.

When everyone is barefoot, say: **Now that we've knocked our socks off, everyone who is barefoot should head back to our lesson.**

37

Together Tag

(You'll need a long rope or some masking tape.)

Say: **Let's take a break from our lesson and play Together Tag.** Lay a rope on the floor to divide the room in half. (Or divide the room using masking tape.) Form two teams. Have the teams stand on opposite sides of the rope.

Explain the rules:

❑ The purpose of the game is to tag children on the opposite side of the rope before getting tagged.

❑ Children must stay on their side of the rope, trying to tag others by reaching across.

❑ Once a child gets tagged, he or she jumps to the other side and joins that team.

❑ On "go," children will start trying to tag opposite team members. An "official tag" occurs when a player touches someone and says "Together Tag" first.

❑ Kids can get in a safety no-tag zone by stepping back from the rope. They can stay back for only three seconds.

Play Together Tag until all the children are on one side. Then say: **Now that we're all together, let's get back to our lesson.**

38

Race for the Frisbee

(You'll need a Frisbee.)

Take children outside to an open area. Give a Frisbee to a volunteer to start the game. Have the volunteer throw it and yell, "Race for the Frisbee!" The other children run after it. The first child to get to the Frisbee picks it up and waits for the other children to get there.

When all the children are together, the child throws the Frisbee in another direction and yells, "Race for the Frisbee!" All the children run after it. There's only one catch: The child who throws the Frisbee can't run until he or she counts to 10 after throwing it. That way other children can have a head start and race to pick it up.

After several throws, say: **Let's catch our breath by getting back to our lesson.**

Hula Hoop Shuffle

(You'll need one or more Hula Hoops.)

Grab kids' attention by rolling out a Hula Hoop. Get as many children as you can to fit inside it while standing. Depending on your group's size, you may need more than one hoop.

Designate one child in each hoop to be "forward." Explain that you'll shout out directions for the Hula Hoops to move. Have the Hula Hoops move forward, backward and sideways.

Call out directions slowly at first, then call out directions more quickly until children either tire out or are laughing so hard they can't move.

Then say: **Let's step out of our hoops and learn more about God's love that encircles us.**

Doctor Says

Choose one child to be the doctor and face the rest of the children. Tell the kids that this game is played like "Simon Says." The doctor will shout out orders preceded by "The doctor says." The doctor can name ailments or check-up procedures, such as:

❑ cough
❑ sneeze
❑ walk with a broken leg
❑ stick out your tongue and say "ah"
❑ rub a bee sting on your arm
❑ gargle

If a child does an action when the doctor doesn't begin with "The doctor says," all the children must rush that child to the hospital (a designated area near the activity) and gently lay the child on the floor. Change doctors after three or four calls. Continue until just one child is left doing the actions.

Then say: **The doctor says it's time for everyone to get back to the lesson.**

41

Scripture Pop-Up

Find a simple Bible verse—or one you're studying—and assign each child a different word from it. If you have a lot of children, give several children the same word.

Have the children mix themselves up and crouch down. As you read the verse, children should each jump up when they hear their word. Then have them quickly crouch down again.

Reread the verse a number of times in several ways—fast, slow, in a high voice, in a low voice. Finally, read the verse and have kids pop up and stand in a line—in order like the verse.

Then say: **Now let's all pop back to our lesson.**

42

Hugs That Count

Say: **I think it's time for a hugging game.** Have children run around the room. When you yell out a number, children form groups of that size and give each other a group hug.

Then break up the hugs and have children run around until you yell another number. At the end, yell the total number of children so they create one large group hug.

Say: **You're great at a group hug! Now show me how great you are at a group lesson.**

43

Turtle Travels

(You'll need a 5×5-foot sheet of cardboard
for every five children.)

Form groups of no more than five children each. Ask each group of children to get on their hands and knees and form a circle with their feet in the center and their heads to the outside. Balance a 5×5-foot piece of cardboard on each group's back—this makes a turtle with a shell. Designate one child in each group to be the head.

Then have turtles travel slowly around the room, being careful not to knock off their shells. At times, yell out "danger!" and have turtles stick their heads into their shells until you say it's safe to proceed.

Play for a while, then take off the turtles' shells. Continue by saying: **Turtles move much too slowly. Let's act like rabbits and hop back to our lesson.**

44

Escape!

Say: **Let's form a big circle and escape from our lesson for a while.** Ask kids to form a circle and stand an arm's length apart. Have one person stand in the middle. Tell the center person to try to escape by running between two children who are part of the circle. Children forming the circle can move closer to the right or left to close a gap that the runner is trying to get through.

When a child escapes, the two children the escapee ran between must chase him or her around the circle. Whoever is last to get around the circle is the next child to be in the center.

Make the game more challenging by letting two people be in the center. Children need to be alert because sometimes the second middle person will escape through the large gap left by the first escapee.

After a while say: **Now let's all escape back to our lesson.**

45

Tightrope Tiptoe

(You'll need a 10- to 25-foot rope.)

Have children form two teams. Lay the rope on the floor in a straight line. Have each team line up on opposite ends of the rope.

Designate one child to start. Have that child tiptoe on the rope, trying not to "fall off." When he or she gets to the end, have the first child of the other team start across. If a child falls off, have him or her start again.

Start out slowly. As children become more confident, encourage them to tiptoe faster. Have a contest to see which team has the most members tiptoe across the tightrope without falling.

Give a cheer for the tightrope tiptoers, then say: **Let's tiptoe back to our lesson.**

Musical Cap

(You'll need a baseball cap and music to play.)

Have children stand in a circle. Give one child a baseball cap. Ask another child to stand in the middle of the circle.

Start the music. Whoever has the cap quickly tosses it to someone else in the circle. The child in the middle tries to intercept the cap as it's being tossed. If he or she succeeds, the child who threw the cap must change places with the child in the middle.

Play for a while, then add another element to the game. When you stop the music, whoever is holding the cap gives it to someone else and joins the person in the middle of the circle. Continue the music, this time playing with two center children trying to intercept the cap toss. Occasionally stop the music and let another person in the center.

After a while, say: **My hat is off to all of you for a great job. Let's cap off this game by getting back to our lesson.**

The Cat's Meow

(You'll need a blindfold.)

Get kids' attention by bringing out the blindfold and tossing it to someone. Blindfold that person, lead him or her to the middle of the room and ask him or her to sit down. Ask the rest of the children to form a circle around the blindfolded child.

Then have the children slowly walk around the blindfolded child. When you say "stop," children must freeze and the blindfolded child points at someone. The child being pointed at must say "Meow."

Give the blindfolded child two chances to guess who the "cat" is. If the blindfolded child is right, he or she changes places with the cat. If the child doesn't guess the cat's identity after two tries, play the game again.

After several children have been blindfolded, have everyone meow as you go back to your meeting area.

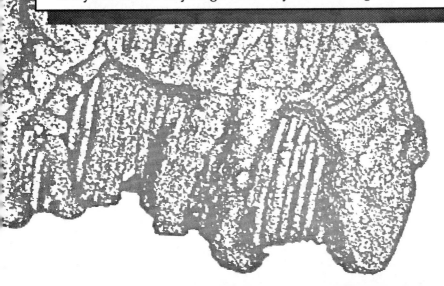

48

Run From the Wicked King

Tell children they're going to run from the wicked king just like the prophet Elijah did. Say: **If you run from the wicked king, you can get away. But you'll have to run through tough spots to escape.** Have children act out these motions with you as if they were running from the wicked king:

- ❑ Climb the palace wall.
- ❑ Tiptoe around a guard.
- ❑ Jump over a trap.
- ❑ Crawl quickly on all fours.
- ❑ Run as fast as you can.
- ❑ Swim across a river.
- ❑ Take some deep breaths.

Say: **Whew! We got away from the wicked king, and so did Elijah. Now let's run back to our lesson and learn more about God's protection and love.**

49

Who Are You?

S ay: **Let's get to know each other better. Let me introduce each of you to the others.**
Ask children to stand in a circle. "Introduce" each child by stomping out each syllable of his or her name. You do the syllable-stomping first, then kids repeat. For example, **This** (stomp) **is** (stomp) **Lin** (stomp) **da** (stomp) **Jones** (stomp).

Children in the circle then wave at Linda and stomp each syllable as they say, "Hi (stomp) Lin (stomp) da (stomp) Jones (stomp)." Continue around the circle until every child has been introduced.

Then say (as you stomp each syllable): **I'm (name), and it's time to stomp back to our lesson.**

Ice-Cube Castles

(You'll need an empty ice-cube tray for every
two children. Food coloring is optional.)

O n a winter day when there's snow on the ground,
use this activity to get outside and play. Have
children bundle up to go outside. Give each pair
of children an empty ice-cube tray. Ask children to pack
snow into their ice-cube trays to make cubes. Then have
all the children work together to build an ice-cube snow
castle. Use food coloring to brighten up the castle if
you'd like.

In a warm climate or in the summer, make cube
sand castles with ice-cube trays and sand.

Then say: **Now that we've built our castles,
let's go back and build on our lesson.**

PART THREE

Fidget Busters for Fourth- to Sixth-Graders

Hat Scramble

(You'll need three pieces of paper and three pencils. You'll also need about 30 different hats, depending on your group's size. Check your own closet for hats, ask kids to wear hats to the lesson or get others from a Salvation Army or Goodwill store.)

Before your lesson, pile the hats on one side of the room. Get kids' attention by saying: **Look at that pile of hats. Let's scramble for those hats by playing a game.**

Form three teams and have each team stand in a line on the side of the room opposite the pile of hats. Ask one person from each team to stand near the pile of hats and count. Give the "counters" each a piece of paper and a pencil to keep track of numbers.

When you say "go," have one child from each team run to the pile of hats and try to put on as many hats at once as is possible. The designated counters each count the number of hats their teammate puts on before the stack of hats falls off. Repeat the activity until every child has tried it. Then add up the scores.

Give a cheer to the winning team, then say: **Now let's scramble to put these hats away and get back to our lesson.**

52

Newspaper Pileup

(You'll need a sheet of newspaper,
a piece of paper and a pencil.)

Interrupt your lesson by putting a large sheet of
newspaper on the floor in the center of the room.
Have kids gather around it. Ask them to predict
how many kids can pile on the sheet of newspaper.
Write the guesses on a piece of paper, keeping track of
who guessed what.

Then have kids try to fit as many people on the
newspaper as possible. Give a group hug to the child
who guessed the closest.

Say: **Now that we all made headlines, let's
get back to our lesson full of good news.**

53

New or Old?

(You'll need a Bible.)

Designate one side of the room to represent "old"
and the other side to represent "new." As you
shout out books of the Bible, have children run
to either side of the room depending on whether they
think the book is in the Old or New Testament. After
each one, have a child check the Bible's table of contents to see who guessed correctly.

Once you've done a number of books (or all of
them), say: **Let's stop this game before it gets old.
Let's study something new in our lesson.**

54

Up in the Air

(You'll need an inflated balloon for every four people.)

Form groups of four and give each group an inflated balloon. Ask one person from each group to hold the balloon above his or her head. On "go," the balloon-holders let go of the balloon. The teams each try to keep their balloon up in the air by blowing it. No one can touch the balloon once it's let go. Compete to see which group can keep the balloon airborne the longest.

Other variations:

❑ Have children use only their heads.

❑ Have children use only their elbows.

❑ Have children lie on their backs and use only their feet.

Say: **Since everything's been up in the air for the past few minutes, let's get our feet on the ground and get back to our lesson.**

55

Spider Web News

(You'll need one or two balls of yarn.)

You can play this affirmation game as one group, or if children feel somewhat uncomfortable with each other, form a group of boys and another group of girls.

Have kids form a circle. Toss a ball of yarn to someone. The yarn-holder wraps the end of the yarn around his or her finger, then throws the ball of yarn to someone else in the circle and gives a compliment; for example, "I like how you're friendly to everyone." That child then wraps the yarn around his or her finger before tossing the ball to another child and giving a compliment. Continue until a large web emerges.

Ask the children to lay the webbed symbols of affirmation on the floor and untangle their fingers.

Then say: **Look at these webs of good news we've heard from each other. You're all wonderful. Now let's go hear some good news in our lesson.**

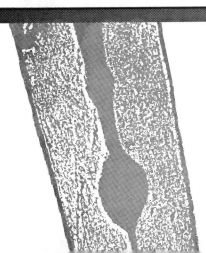

The Hero

Ask for a volunteer and call him or her the "seeker." Have the seeker leave the room. Ask for another volunteer and call that person the "hero."

Bring the seeker back into the room. Explain that he or she will walk around while children move around the room. When the seeker gets close to the child designated the hero, have children clap, cheer and say, "Hip, hip, hooray!" When the seeker moves away from the hero, have the children cheer and applaud more quietly. The closer the seeker gets to the hero, the louder the cheers become. When the seeker picks the right person as the hero, play the game again with a new seeker and hero.

Then say: **Now let's seek out our lesson,** and have children clap and cheer louder and louder as you go back to your meeting area.

The Samaritan Shuffle

(You'll need eight balloons with slips of paper
in them as described. You'll also need a Bible.)

In advance, write events from the parable of the
good Samaritan (Luke 10:30-37) on slips of paper,
one for each balloon. For example:

❑ Man walks from Jerusalem to Jericho.
❑ Robbers attack and beat up the man.
❑ A priest walks past the wounded man.
❑ A Levite walks past the wounded man.
❑ A Samaritan stops to bandage the man's wounds.
❑ A Samaritan puts the wounded man onto an
animal.
❑ A Samaritan takes the wounded man to a motel.
❑ A Samaritan pays the motel manager to take care
of the hurt man.

Put one slip of paper into each balloon and inflate
the balloons. Have children form a circle and bat the
balloons around. When you yell "Stop and pop!" children grab a balloon, pop it and retrieve the slip of paper.
Have children figure out the correct sequence of the
parable without looking at the Bible. Then read Luke
10:30-37 aloud to see how they did.

Say: **It's time to be good, listening Samar-
itans, so let's quietly tiptoe back to our lesson.**

58

Tug of Winners

(You'll need a 10-foot rope.)

Form two teams and have each team line up on either end of a 10-foot rope as if they were going to play Tug of War. Instead, play Tug of Winners, a game in which the two teams try to get into a rhythm of seesawing back and forth with the rope. Once children get the rhythm, have them seesaw:

❏ slowly   ❏ as if they were in a wind storm
❏ quickly   ❏ as if they were in a hot desert

Conclude by having both teams slowly seesaw back and forth as they go back to your meeting area.

59

Card Grab

(You'll need a 3×5 card and tape for each child.)

Tape a 3×5 card to each child's back. Have children try to grab other kids' cards while protecting their own. When children grab someone's card, they must stick it on their own back. When children lose their own card, they continue trying to get other people's cards. The child who has the most cards when you call time wins.

Say: **Now let's grab for our lesson.**

Fill Noah's Ark

(You'll need three empty margarine tubs, about 75 slips of paper and three markers or pens. You'll also need snacks, such as animal crackers, Teddy Grahams or fish crackers.)

Form three teams. Have them line up on one side of the room. Give each team about 25 slips of paper and a marker or pen. At the other side of the room, place an empty margarine tub for each team.

Explain that each team should fill its margarine tub (which you call Noah's ark) with as many different animals as the team can name. Team members take turns writing an animal's name on a slip of paper and then running to the team's Noah's ark to deposit the slip. Team members can help each other think of animals; however, teams can have only one runner going at a time. When a runner returns, another child may run to the ark to drop in an animal's name.

Play for about five minutes. At the end, count the number of animals in each ark, discarding any duplicates within the ark. Announce the winning team by awarding them the animal crackers, Teddy Grahams or fish crackers. Have them serve the other children, then let everyone munch the goodies.

After the snack time, say: **Now that we've filled up the ark and filled up our stomachs, let's fill up our minds with knowledge from our lesson.**

The Active Alphabet

(You'll need chalk and a chalkboard. You'll also need two
Bibles with dictionaries and concordances.)

Form two teams and give each team a Bible. Show
the teams where to find the table of contents,
dictionary and concordance in their Bibles. Tell
kids they can use these tools to help them during the
game.

Have the two teams stand single file about 20 feet
from a chalkboard. When you say "go," the first player
in each line runs to the chalkboard and writes a biblical
place or person's name beginning with the letter A,
such as Absalom or Abraham. The child then runs back
and tags the next person who runs to the board and
writes a biblical name or place starting with a B, such as
Bethlehem or Bathsheba. Continue through the entire
alphabet. Team members who played earlier rejoin the
line so a team always has enough runners.

Team members can help each other in thinking of
names and places. Make the game more challenging by
having kids spell the names and places correctly. Also, if
one team thinks up a name or place for a certain letter,
the other team can't use the same one.

After going through the alphabet, say: **Let's brush
up on our Bible ABCs by getting back to our
lesson.**

62

Mail Jumble

(You'll need a large collection of unopened mail in a box.
You'll also need four empty boxes and a map or globe.)

S how kids the unopened mail in a box. Have them
work together to figure out how many states,
provinces or countries the mail came from.
Then designate the four sides of the room to represent north, south, east and west. Put a box at each lo-
cation. Bring out the map or globe and ask someone to
point to your town. Let everyone see. Point out north,
south, east and west on the map or globe. Then have
children "deliver" the mail to the direction (in relation
to your town) where the mail came from. See how
quickly they can deliver the mail.
Then say: **Let's leave this jumble of mail and
get back to reading something really important:
our lesson.**

63

Leaf Our Pile Alone!

(You'll need several rakes, one rope, and nametags made
from red and blue construction paper. Play outside in
an area that has lots of leaves on the ground.)

Form two teams to play this game outside in the
fall. Give red nametags to team members in one
group and blue nametags to the other team
members.

Have each team rake a pile of leaves on opposite
ends of a field, park or playing area. Put a rope on the
ground dividing the two teams.

When stacks are complete, tell kids these rules:

❑ The red team will start out guarding its pile of
leaves.

❑ The blue team runs to the red team's pile of leaves
and tries to jump in the pile before getting tagged.

❑ If a child is tagged, he or she must sit out and
cheer his or her team.

❑ Count the number of blue team members who
succeeded in jumping in the pile of leaves.

❑ Then switch. Blue team members guard their pile
while the red team tries to jump in their leaves.

❑ Count the number of red team members in the
pile of leaves. The winning team is the team that gets
the most players in the other team's pile.

Once a team is declared a winner, have all the children jump into the piles of leaves. Then say: **Let's leaf
this game and get back to our lesson.**

(You can play this game inside any time of the year
by having kids make two piles of crumpled newspaper
wads. Play by the same rules!)

Coupon Discovery

(You'll need a bucket. For each child, you'll need
scissors and a coupon insert from a Sunday paper.)

This game will sharpen kids' thinking and let
them run off energy at the same time. Give each
child scissors and a coupon insert. As children
cut out their coupons, place a bucket about 20 feet
away. When you yell out certain aspects of a coupon,
children must quickly sort through their coupons, find
the coupon that represents what you're calling for and
run to the bucket to place that coupon inside.

Yell out aspects such as:

❏ the closest expiration date
❏ the furthest expiration date
❏ the smallest coupon value
❏ the largest coupon value

Then say: **Good job examining those valuable
coupons. Let's all run and drop our remaining
coupons into the bucket before examining our
valuable lesson.**

65

Group Basketball

(You'll need old newspapers and some masking tape.)

Form two teams and use masking tape to mark a line on the floor to separate them. Have one team hold hands and form a circle. The edge of the circle should be about one foot from the line.

Have the other team stay behind the line. Place a stack of newspapers behind team members. When you say "go," have the team not in a circle wad the newspaper into balls and try to throw them into the circle of children without stepping over the line. The circle team can try to deflect the balls with their bodies, but may not move their hands or feet. After two minutes, count the balls that made it into the circle.

Then have the teams change roles. Continue the activity, having each circle move farther from the line. After you've played several rounds, say: **Now that we've hooped it up for a while, let's get back to the lesson.**

Magazine Madness

(You'll need six paper grocery bags, two marked
"A-H," two marked "I-P" and two marked "Q-Z."
You'll also need old magazines.)

Try a little rip-apart fun with Magazine Madness.
Form two teams and give each team several magazines to rip apart and a set of bags. Place the
bags about 20 feet away from each team.

Tell children that when they see a picture, they
should rip it out, shout the main item pictured, figure
out which letter of the alphabet the item starts with,
and run to put the picture in the appropriate bag. For
example, a picture of a car begins with C and would be
placed in the bag marked "A-H."

After five minutes, have the teams count the number of pictures in their bags. The team with the most
pictures wins. Then say: **Let's give a big cheer for
finding so many pictures! Now let's give a big
cheer for our lesson before getting back to it.**

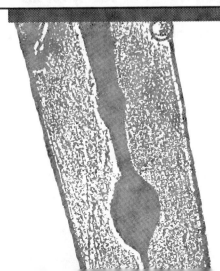

Watermelon Wobble

(You'll need two watermelons, two chairs,
a knife and napkins.)

S how kids the watermelons, then say: **After we
race with these melons we'll eat them up
as our prize.**

Form two equal-size teams. Put a chair about 20
feet in front of each team. Give each team a watermelon.

Have all team members get on their hands and
knees and form a single line. When you say "go," have
the first member from each team roll the watermelon to
the chair, around it and back without getting off his or
her hands and knees. Then the next team member rolls
the watermelon around the chair and back.

After everyone has completed the course, eat the
watermelons. Then say: **Let's wash our sticky hands
and then let's stick to our lesson.**

Beach Ball Bounce

(You'll need two beach towels and a beach ball.)

Throw a beach towel to a person on one side of the room; throw another beach towel to a person on the other side of the room. Form two equal-size teams by having kids get with the beach towel-holder closest to them. Have team members surround their towel and hold it taut.

Then give one team a beach ball. Have that team use the taut towel to toss the beach ball to the other team. That team should try to catch the ball with its towel. See how many times teams can toss the ball back and forth without dropping it. Start out with teams close together, then move farther apart.

Then say: **We had a ball with that activity. Now let's have a ball with our lesson.**

69

Ping-Pong Blow

(You'll need several Ping-Pong balls.)

I f kids look like they need to blow off some steam, this activity should blow them away. Have children form a circle lying on their stomachs with their heads facing center. Give one child a Ping-Pong ball. Have children keep the ball moving across the circle by blowing it.

If you have more than six children, form smaller circles so the ball doesn't get stuck in the middle. Have kids take breaks so they don't get lightheaded.

After a while, have kids blow the balls toward your meeting area, then continue your lesson.

70

Look at That Face!

S top the lesson and say: **Turn to a person sitting close to you.** Make sure everyone finds a partner. Have the partner who ate breakfast the earliest be the "mirror." The other child then makes faces for the mirror to copy. After a few minutes, switch so the other partner can be the mirror.

Then make the activity more complicated by having one partner make contorted faces and body shapes at the same time. See how well the mirrors can keep up. See how long it takes for everyone to start laughing.

End the activity by saying: **Now everyone mirror me as I go back to study the lesson.**

71

Crazy Circles

(You'll need snacks shaped like circles,
such as doughnuts or bagels.)

Have children stand in the center of the room. When you yell out a question, children must quickly find out which group they fit in and form a circle. For example, when you call out "Which month were you born in?" all kids with January birthdays would form a circle, and so on.

Call out questions, such as:

❑ Which month were you born in?
❑ How many children are in your family?
❑ How many pets do you have?
❑ What's your favorite subject in school?

End by asking: **Now who's in the fourth to sixth grade? All of you? Good! Now let's form one big circle and finish our lesson.**

Sit in the circle while you complete your lesson. Serve scrumptious snacks shaped like circles, such as doughnuts or bagels.

Pass the Balloons

(You'll need several inflated balloons.
Place them in a large trash bag.)

G et kids' attention by bringing out one balloon and leading children to form a circle. Have them each face the back of the person on their right. Give one child the balloon to pass over his or her head to the child behind. That child then passes the balloon through his or her legs to the next child. Continue the over-and-under passing all around the circle.

Gradually add more balloons until the passing gets crazy. Then say: **Let's pop all the balloons before getting back to our lesson.**

Water Balloon Bust

(You'll need a water balloon for each child.)

T his activity works well outside on a hot day. Say: **Follow me for a cooling-off game.** Once you're outside, have children form a circle. Give each child a water balloon. Have children slowly pass the water balloons around the circle clockwise. Gradually speed up the process. Then have each person take a step back. If you wish, reverse the flow from time to time to add to the confusion.

See how long it takes for all the balloons to burst. Then say: **I don't mean to water down your fun, but I'm bursting to get back to the lesson.**

Runaway Crabs

(You'll need pillows or mats to make
a soft area on the floor.)

Ask kids to follow you to the soft area you have prepared on the floor. Form two teams: the crabs and
the crab-catchers. Children who are crabs must
crawl on their hands and feet with their backs toward
the floor. Crab-catchers can run and walk.

Have crab-catchers work in pairs to pick up crabs
(with one child holding a crab's feet and the other
holding the crab's hands) and carry them to the soft
area. As soon as the crab-catchers gently put a crab into
the soft area, have them run out and catch another
crab. The only problem is that as soon as crabs have
been placed on the soft area, they can crawl away to
escape. After you've played a few minutes, switch roles
so the crabs can be crab-catchers and vice versa.

Stop playing before children get "crabby" with this
chaotic game. Then say: **Let's not get crabby. Let's
snap back to our lesson.**

Daniel and the Lions

Get kids ready for a roaring good time with this game. Choose one child to be Daniel. Have the other children be lions. Explain these rules:

❏ The lions try to tag Daniel, but lions can only tag Daniel from behind, not from the side or from the front.

❏ Daniel, however, can tag the others in any direction.

❏ If Daniel tags a lion first, the lion becomes a guardian angel and can help Daniel tag other lions. Lions can only tag guardian angels from behind.

❏ The lions roar during the game.

❏ If a lion tags Daniel, that lion becomes the new Daniel and play continues.

Keep playing until Daniel and his guardian angels have tagged all the lions. Then say: **Let's all roar together and run back to our lesson.**

Twisted Giggles

Have children take off their shoes and stand close together. Explain that you'll give them instructions on how to connect their feet, hands and elbows with other children. Explain that they should touch as many different children as they can.

Then say:

- ❑ Have your right foot touch someone's left foot.
- ❑ Have your right hand hold someone else's right hand.
- ❑ Have your left hand touch somebody's knee.
- ❑ Move your right hand to touch someone's head.
- ❑ Have your left elbow touch somebody's leg.
- ❑ Have your right elbow touch one of your legs.

Say: **What a twisted mess! Let's get untwisted, put on our shoes and go straight back to our lesson.**

Pillars and Runners

Tell kids it's time for a break. Have them spread out and wander around the room. When you shout out descriptions, have all the kids who *do* fit the description freeze in place like pillars. Have those who *do not* fit the description run around the room, weaving in and out of the pillars. When kids are almost done weaving, switch to another description so that different kids freeze while others weave.

Yell descriptions, such as:

❏ 9-year-olds
❏ 10-year-olds
❏ 11-year-olds
❏ Has a brother
❏ Has a sister
❏ Is an only child
❏ Has black hair
❏ Has brown eyes
❏ Likes math

For variation and added excitement, mix in some descriptions that fit all the kids, such as "is in church" and some that fit none of the kids, such as "is 10 feet tall."

After a while, get everyone to freeze by saying: **Is having fun. Now let's learn more about our lesson.**

PART FOUR
Fidget Busters for Children of All Ages

Follow the Chalk

(You'll need four different colors of chalk.)

Form groups of four. Give one child in each group a piece of white chalk. Give each of the other three children a piece of different-color chalk. Then, have the groups follow you outdoors. (If the weather is too cold, play this game indoors using several chalkboards.)

On the sidewalk, parking lot or driveway, have children with the white chalk begin to draw on the pavement. Encourage them to intersect each other's lines.

Then have the other children in each group follow their leader's lines by drawing alongside the white line with their colored chalk. This gets tricky and funny if you have a lot children.

After the pavement is covered with an array of colors, stop the game. Have children all survey their artwork and cheer. Then say: **Let's chalk one up for a fun activity and get back to our lesson.**

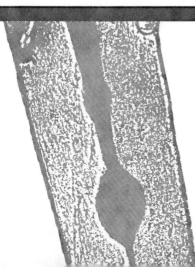

Chain of Events

This easy activity is like Follow the Leader—with a delayed reaction. You be first in line. Have the children line up single file behind you and each hold the waist of the person in front of them.

Tell kids they must each do the same action as the person in front of them, but they can't do the action until after that person actually does it. You do different actions for people to follow, such as squatting, skipping, jumping, walking while bent over, shaking your head or wiggling. Start a second action before the whole line finishes the first one. Change the line leader and let others think of actions to pass down the line.

Then say: **Now let's follow the leader back to our lesson.** Have the leader take the children back to the lesson area.

Magnetic Force

(If you do this activity with preschoolers, bring
a magnet and a few metal paper clips to class
so you can demonstrate what a magnet does.)

Tell the group that you're going to play an energizing activity. Explain to younger preschool
children that magnets attract or draw certain
things toward them. Show them how a magnet attracts
metal paper clips. Tell kids that they're going to play a
game and act like magnets.

When you shout out an instruction, all the children who fit that description must act like magnets and
race together to form a tight bunch. Have the rest of the
children jump up and down and cheer for the "magnetic" group. The group disbands when you call out
another instruction, and a new magnetic force comes
together. Call out descriptions, such as:

❏ everyone who's wearing blue socks
❏ everyone who's wearing jeans
❏ everyone who's got two eyes
❏ everyone who watched television last night
❏ everyone who has a dog
❏ everyone who likes pizza

Then say: **I feel something pulling me back
to the lesson. Let's all stick together in a group
and inch our way back to our seats.**

Tickle Toes

I f you're having trouble with children giggling during a class, take advantage of their funny bones
with this "laughable" fidget buster.

Have children take off their shoes and form a circle
by lying head to foot on their backs. The feet of one
child should be next to the head of the next child. (Be
sensitive to fifth- and sixth-grade boys who may be
hesitant to participate. Let them serve as helpers.)

Have children each grab the feet of the child lying
ahead of them. On the count of three, children should
all gently tickle the feet they're holding. Then have kids
each rotate 180 degrees to tickle the feet of the person
on their other side. Go back and forth as much as you
want with this toe-tickling activity.

When kids are giggled out, say: **Now that we've
all gotten the giggles out, let's get serious about
our lesson.**

Hats Off

(You'll need a hat for each child, except for one. If you can't find that many hats, have kids make them by rolling construction paper into cone shapes and taping them.)

Give each child a hat except for one. When you yell "hats off," have all children throw their hats into the air, then scramble to get another hat. The one who doesn't get a hat must choose one hat from another child and sit out along the side. That child then yells, "hats off" to play the activity again. Continue playing until you're down to one child.

Then say: **Hats off to each one of you. Now let's put our thinking caps on as we learn more about Jesus.**

Race Around

When children's attention seems to be running in different directions, have them run to different places to burn off some energy.

If you do this activity indoors, clear the area for children to run safely. If you're outside, make sure the area is self-contained and far from traffic.

Call out a place or object for the entire group to race to, such as a garbage can. Once children race to the object, choose another for them to run to, such as the chalkboard. Continue the activity until children start to slow down.

As the last instruction, say: **Now let's race to our seats to continue our lesson.**

Parking Lot Painting

(You'll need a small paper cup for
each child and buckets of water.)

On a hot summer day, take children outside to the
parking lot. Give each child a small paper cup
full of water. Have buckets of water nearby for
refills. Encourage children to "paint" on the parking lot
by carefully pouring water from their cups. Tell them
they shouldn't be too slow, because water evaporates
quickly.

Younger children can create simple water designs.
Encourage older children to work together to create
complex mazes or scenes.

Allow time for kids to admire each other's paint-
ings, then say: **Let's all paint a water trail to the
door so we can get back to our lesson.**

Musical Circle

(You'll need music.)

If kids are tuning out of your lesson, say: **I have an idea that'll be music to your ears. Let's play a musical game.**

Have children hold hands and form a circle. Choose one child to stand in the middle of the circle and be "It."

Play music and have children in the circle skip. When the music stops, have children in the circle sit down before "It" tags someone. If "It" tags someone first, "It" joins the circle, and the child who was tagged goes to the middle to repeat the process. If "It" doesn't tag anyone, he or she stays in the center for another turn.

After playing several times, say: **Let's stop the music and get back to our noteworthy lesson.**

86

Animal Run

Have children line up along a wall. Explain that you're having a race to the opposite side of the room, and the children must run like the animal you shout out.

During the race, when you shout an animal name, children must immediately change how they're running. Consider using these animals:

❑ kangaroo   ❑ crab   ❑ rabbit
❑ snake   ❑ monkey   ❑ turtle

When everyone has finished the race, say: **Let's all act like birds and fly back to our lesson.**

87

Small, Smaller, Smallest

Have children cover their eyes while you choose an object in the room. Then have children open their eyes and walk around the room searching for the item. Give hints about which child is closest, such as "Gina is getting closer." Continue giving hints until a child chooses the right object.

Then that child will secretly choose a smaller object for others to guess. Continue playing until you get to an extremely small object, such as a thumbtack.

Then say: **Now we have something big to find: our lesson. Let's go!**

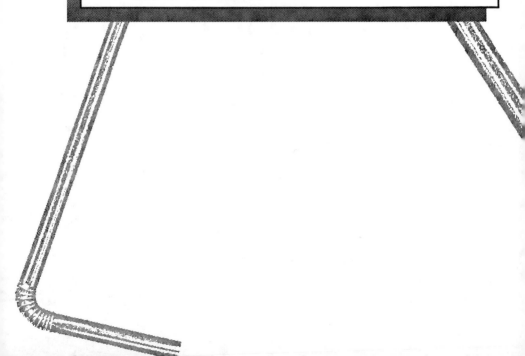

88

Who Left?

S ay: **Let's stop for a few minutes and play a game called Who Left?** Depending on how well your children know each other, you may need to go over everyone's name before playing this game.

Choose one child to be "It" and to close his or her eyes. Meanwhile, walk over to another child and whisper in his or her ear to leave the room for a few seconds until you say for him or her to come back in.

Ask "It" to uncover his or her eyes and guess within five seconds who left. If he or she guesses correctly, the child who left becomes "It."

For older children, make the activity more challenging by having several children leave (without telling "It" how many left).

Then say: **Let's all uncover our eyes for a better look at our lesson.**

Nose to Nose

(You'll need two identical sets of 3×5 cards with a body part written on each one. Make enough cards so each child has one. Use parts such as foot, hand, elbow, knee, hip, back, shoulder, wrist and ankle. Turn the cards upside down and keep the two sets separate. For younger children, draw the body parts.)

Take time out from your lesson for this toe-tapping, fidget-busting activity. Form two equal-size teams and have each team stand in single file at one end of the room. Place the card sets in separate stacks on the floor about 20 feet from the teams.

Explain that they'll have a relay race where one child from each team must run to pick one card, read it (or see what body part is drawn on it), and then run back to tag the next child with and on the body part mentioned on the card. For example, if the card says "knee," the child must tag the next person in line by having his or her knee tag the next child's knee.

After completing the relay, say: **Let's give ourselves a hand before getting back to our lesson.**

90

Peanut Hunt

(You'll need unshelled peanuts and paper cups.)

Hide a large number of unshelled peanuts around the room before children arrive. When kids are about to drive you nuts with fidgeting, give them each a paper cup. Then have a peanut hunt. Tell children to quickly find as many peanuts as possible. After children find most of the peanuts, have a shelling-and-eating party. Have a bag of peanuts on hand and fill up kids' cups so that everyone has several to munch on.

Then say: **This activity was fun, but nutty. Let's do something less crazy like getting back to our lesson.**

91

Giggle-Busters

Say: **Stand up and take a stretch.** Tell kids that when you yell "giggle," they'll start laughing. After a few seconds, you'll yell "stop!" and then everyone has to keep a perfectly straight face. Keep signaling "giggle" and "stop" until everyone's laughing and tuckered out.

Then say: **Now that we're all giggled out, let's take a deep breath and get back to our lesson.**

Where in the Church?

(You'll need pictures of items around your church, such as an organ, piano, kitchen, hymnal, altar and pew. Cut them out of religious magazines or take instant-print pictures around your own church. Place the pictures in a box.)

When you want to stretch kids' legs, take a church tour with this activity. Bring out the box filled with pictures. Ask: **Where in the church can we find this item?** Take the box with you and go as a group to the item. Draw out another picture and continue your tour to the next church object.

Make the activity more challenging for older children by forming two teams. Have each team choose a picture from the box. Teams must then run and find the item. Once each child from the team has touched the item, have the team run back to pull out a picture of another object to find. Caution children to be as quiet as possible if other classes are meeting at the same time.

Once all the items have been found and all the children have returned from their hunt, say: **Now where in the church were we studying our lesson? Let's get back to it!**

Body Bunches

(You'll need bunches of grapes.)

Stop your lesson and say: **Body bunch! Body bunch! Make groups of three!** Help children form groups of three. Then have them touch each other in their bunches with only the body part you name. For example:

- ❑ hands
- ❑ feet
- ❑ elbows
- ❑ toes
- ❑ knees
- ❑ rears
- ❑ heads
- ❑ wrists
- ❑ hips

After you name three or four body-bunching body parts, shout: **Body bunch! Body bunch! Make new groups of four!** Shout out three or four more body-bunching body parts. Repeat the activity with groups of five. Then six. Then say: **Let's form one big bunch and shuffle back to our lesson.**

Serve bunches of grapes for a snack.

94

Do What I Do

Interrupt your lesson and say to the children: **Do what I do.** Then lead them in actions, such as marching in place, waving your hand, stomping your feet, scratching your head and circling your arms.

Then say: **Do what I do. Follow me and let's form a circle.** Once you're in the circle, point to someone else to be the leader. He or she says, "Do what I do" as he or she does an action. Actions can be as simple as clapping hands and doing the twist, or as zany as touching your tongue to your nose.

End the copy-cat time by saying, "Do what I do" as you lead everyone back to their seats.

95

Stone Faces

Have kids form a circle. Choose one child to be "It" and stand in the center of the circle. Ask everyone else to be quiet and keep a serious "stone" face. Have "It" go around the circle making faces, trying to make others laugh or smile—no tickling or touching allowed. When kids smile or laugh, they join "It" in the middle and help make other children break their stone faces.

After everyone has laughed or smiled, say: **Now that we've had a good laugh, let's keep smiling as we go back to our exciting lesson.**

If the Shoe Fits

(You'll need shoestring potatoes or string licorice for snacks.)

Say: **Oh, my aching feet. I need to wiggle my toes and relax a bit. Let's play a game and give our feet a break.**

Form groups of five. Have the children in each group take off their shoes, pile them up and mix them. Have each group stand in a circle around the shoes and hold hands.

On "go," group members each can "pick up" a shoe (not their own) by sliding their feet into it and passing it clockwise around the circle. The shoes continue around the circle until they reach their owners. As soon as a team gets the shoes back to their owners, kids can drop hands and put them back on.

Make this "shoe-win" activity more difficult. Allow no talking.

Then say: **Now let's get on with the shoe—our lesson!** Serve shoestring potatoes or string licorice for a snack.

97

The Long Tunnel

(You'll need a beach ball or basketball.)

Say: **Tunnel time! Tunnel time! Time to form a tunnel.** Show children how they can form a tunnel by standing in a single line with their legs spread apart. Start rolling a beach ball or basketball between the first person's legs through the tunnel. Let children help steer the ball to keep it going.

Once the ball goes through a child's legs, he or she must run to the end of the line to extend the tunnel. See how long the group can keep the ball going. Then say: **Now that we've all had a ball, let's get back to our lesson.**

98

Joyful Jog

Say: **Let's loosen up our legs and take a joyful jog.** Jog around the block or the building with the children. As you jog, have children name things aloud that they're thankful for; for example, trees, cats, flowers, mailboxes, homes and windows.

Then say: **Now let's jog our memories by getting back to our lesson.**

Sponge Carry

(You'll need an inner tube for every three children and a
bunch of yellow, green, blue and pink sponges.)

Help children form groups of three. Give each
group an inner tube and ask members to
squeeze inside of it.

Pile the blue sponges in one corner of the room,
green sponges in another corner, pink sponges in the
third corner and yellow sponges in the remaining corner.

As you yell out a sponge color, teams must rush to
the pile and pick up one sponge. Tube teams can bump
other teams and try to get them to drop their sponges,
so encourage children to pick up a sponge and then
rush quickly away from the pile to avoid getting
bumped. (If teams drop their sponges, they must pick
them up before getting the next color of sponge you
call.)

After teams each pick up a sponge, yell out another
color so teams rush to another corner of the room. Continue yelling out colors until you run out of sponges.
Then say: **We've done enough bumping around,
now let's all act like sponges and soak up our
lesson.**

Over and Under, Around and Through

Tell children to skip or gallop around the room until you yell out a direction. Children must then find a partner and do the action together. Call out directions, such as:

❏ **over your partner** (For example: One child lies down and the other steps over him or her.)

❏ **under your partner** (For example: One child spreads his or her legs and the other one crawls under.)

❏ **around your partner** (For example: One child stands still and the other one runs around him or her.)

Make the game more challenging for older children by having them form groups of four or five. Call out directions, such as:

❏ **through** (For example: Three children line up and spread their legs while another child crawls through the legs of the three children.)

❏ **out** (For example: Four children hold hands in a circle and another child stands outside the circle.)

❏ **up** (For example: Three children lift a child.)

Then say: **Now that we've been up and down and over, we're through with this game. So let's skip back to our lesson.**

Quick Splash

(You'll need a small paper cup of water for each child.)

Use this activity on a hot day when kids are acting like your lesson is a bit too "dry." Go outside and ask children to line up along one side of a grassy area. Give each child a small paper cup filled to the brim with water. On "go," everyone races to the other side of the yard and back—trying not to spill water out of their cups. Compare cups to see who has the most water left. Then say "Cheers" and let kids drink the rest of their water.

Add some more Quick Splash challenge for older children. Ask them each to find a partner. Give each child a paper cup full of water. Ask partners to face each other. Then have a showdown to see which person can be the last person to throw water on his or her partner (but not in the eyes). Partners should try to fool each other into thinking they're about to throw the water first.

After everyone gets wet, have kids pretend to swim back to your meeting area to continue the lesson.